CW01176361

The furniture of
Ed Cruikshank

{pfe}

To my mother Patricia

for giving me wings

and to my love Tonya

for helping me use them.

Copyright 2017 © Ed Cruikshank

Published by
Pause for Effect Limited
PO Box 108, Kingston, OTAGO, New Zealand 9749
All rights reserved.

Without limiting the rights under copyright reserved above, no part of this publication may be reproduced, stored in or introduced into a retrieval system, or transmitted, in any form or by any means (electronic, mechanical, photocopying, recording or otherwise), without the prior written permission of the copyright owner.

Pause for Effect books are available through most book stores and are also available in a variety of electronic formats.

To contact Pause for Effect directly write to: info@pauseforeffect.co.nz

ISBN 978-0-9876653-5-5

Edited by Emma-Kate Moore
Book design by Patrick Dodson
Photography by Michael Thomas, David Comer, Martin Kohn and Patrick Dodson

Printed and bound in the US, UK and Australia by Lightning Source.
Lightning Source UK Ltd. Chapter House, Pitfield, Kiln Farm, Milton Keynes, MK11 3LW.
Email: enquiries@lightningsource.co.uk
Voice: 0845 121 4567. Fax: 0845 121 4594

National Library of New Zealand data (Te Puna Matauranga o Aotearoa):
Title: Ed Cruikshank - A Retrospective of Bespoke Furniture Design
Author: Patrick Dodson
Publisher: Pause for Effect
Address: PO Box 108, Kingston, OTAGO, New Zelaland 9748
Format: Hardback
Publication Date: 10/2017
ISBN: 978-0-9876653-5-5

First Edition

The Furniture of Ed Cruikshank

{pfe}

Foreword

David Linley
London
February 2018

I am very touched to be asked to write the foreword to this wonderful book. Harry worked with Ed for many years it gave me great pleasure to watch his style and skills mature. His professionalism and attention to details are paramount to his art and Craft. I established Linley with the invention of preserving and discovering traditional wood working techniques combined with contemporary design based on historical proportion and its fabulous to See Ed Creating such original and thought provoking Ideas and design.

David Linley.

1

Introduction

Forty thousand years ago, a small band of people found their way into the entrance of a cave on the side of a mountain in what today is Northern Spain. Carrying stone lamps in their hands, burning white deer tallow with juniper wicks, the warm light danced on the cave walls creating bison, auroch, and deer in the flickering shadows. On a long white expanse of wall they stopped, drew powered red ochre from their leather pouches, put it in their mouths, put a hand against the white wall and blew – capturing their hands, that moment, and time itself on a cave wall where it has quietly held the anonymous memory of that moment for thousands and thousands of years.

On the other side of the world, as El Castillo's exact antipodes is modern day New Zealand, a kauri seedling had opened up on the same day, rooted in the soft duff of another giant who had fallen before it. Standing small among its own ancestors, the seedling of 40,000 years ago took root, grew tall and in time, thick trunked and heavy. Each year its heartwood grew and the rings that counted the circles of season pressed closely against each other, leaving a tree who could later be read as a history book of its times. Standing for more than a millennium, it eventually fell and was buried in a swamp, where it was preserved with the same sort of accidental perfection as the handprints of El Castillo. Both cross enormous spans of time. Both invite us to want to touch.

Today, a dark honeyed slab from the fallen kauri greets visitors to the Louis Vuitton shop on Queenstown's waterfront. In the hands of furniture designer, Ed Cruikshank, it has transformed to a table where visitors cannot resist running their hands along its smoothness to feel its depth. They ask to hear its story. See things of timeless beauty resting on it and marvel that it has come from so deep a past to be here now, alive in this incarnation of form and beauty, full of its own past and welcoming the creation of new stories still to be told.

Cruikshank's work as a designer speaks to a rare modern interest in the endurance of time. In a world of speed, disposability, and temporality, Cruikshank takes a very different approach. His design eye is located many years from now. Not in a futuristic Jetson's reality of synthetics, chrome and an imagined life on a planet beyond this one, but of the stories a piece of furniture will know

and hold centuries from now. He is a man interested in family, intimacies, and the power and strength of the domestic as a source of rootedness and joy. Cruikshank works in leather, fur, metal, and wood, seeking out materials like the 40,000 year old swamp kauri, or a pair of Southland beech stumps that have become coffee tables grounding the same space as the kauri table with a warmth and familiarity that tells visitors that they are here, in New Zealand, and that the history of this land can be told in the worn rings of a soft beech tree. That beech tree's stump is a place where you can stop, rest, look to the mountains, and contemplate the nature of time. Even in the midst of a modern shop. Especially there.

Our ochre handed painters in El Castillo would have understood and appreciated the power and simplicity of a pair of tree trunks that were now serving as tables. Their beauty natural and appreciated. Their usefulness eternally assured.

Not all of Cruikshank's pieces are so raw and organic, but each one engages with questions of time, place, relationships, and intention. The materiality of the piece, like an artefact from the past, takes the object beyond form and function to add another element. Each piece has its own mana, a power of story latent within it, because each piece has been created with purpose and for someone specific. This, too, is an unexpected magic in modern times.

Leslie Van Gelder
June 2017
(continued on the last page of the book)

A Retrospective

Every piece of furniture tells a story, has a lineage. Embedded within the design of each object are historical tells, bits of information about the interactions of people in a given period of time, their values and the materials they had access to. So too, then, does a range of furniture tell the larger story of the times; present and past. These stories reveal as much about the designers as they do about the ones being designed for - influenced by inherited styles, the economy, ego, practical need or whimsy. Any given exposure to furniture of today, in say, a showroom, the internet or this book, will at first glance appear as a discreet collection of functional items made for the 'now'. Looking more closely though, the larger story comes into focus. One piece may be the product of 21st century price conscious manufacturing while another piece looks (and probably feels) as though it was deigned for the ages. All in all, every sketch, CAD drawing, material source, machine cut, build and finish will be the product of many stories coming together. What distinguishes one piece of furniture from another is the heritage it adheres to.

The design narrative Ed Cruikshank embraces comes from a time almost lost on many furniture designers today. His education and practice have been grounded in an aesthetic (visual and practical) that listens closely to a history where the details of design and production were so painstakingly applied that each chair, table, sideboard or bed became a piece of highly functional art, made to last hundreds of years (at least) so that the story of the piece and persons, would endure. In today's design and manufacturing milieu - where getting the most stuff for the cheapest price determines design, materials and quality, the idea of a bespoke piece of furniture intentionally made to outlive its owners - creating value and joy for generations - is an uncanny thing. A thing, nevertheless, Cruikshank strives to achieve. The ability to see back through time and appreciate the values of 17th century masters right through to functional modernists is what enables Cruikshank to make products that stand upon these stories while adding his own distinct sense of form, beauty and quality. To Cruikshank, this is the basis of enduring design.

To understand the work before you here - both the initial appearance and the hidden infrastructure - we need to look back through those stories and unpack various movements, economies, personalities and technologies. Parsing out what the designer had to work with and who they were working for gives us a long lens with which to focus in on the details of what constitutes an enduring piece today. For instance when the sawing technologies of the 1500's limited furniture makers to the larger planks of huge oak trees, the resulting long stout rectangular tables or massive four poster beds became great sturdy things made typically by nameless 'house carpenters' who received little or no credit for their craft. The ones commissioning the chunky pieces of this era had a strong if not controlling influence on the overall design and application. The Tudors during this 'Age of Oak' often borrowed from the previous gothic period and moved furniture design in general towards an English renaissance, largely in the service of their own vision. The designers

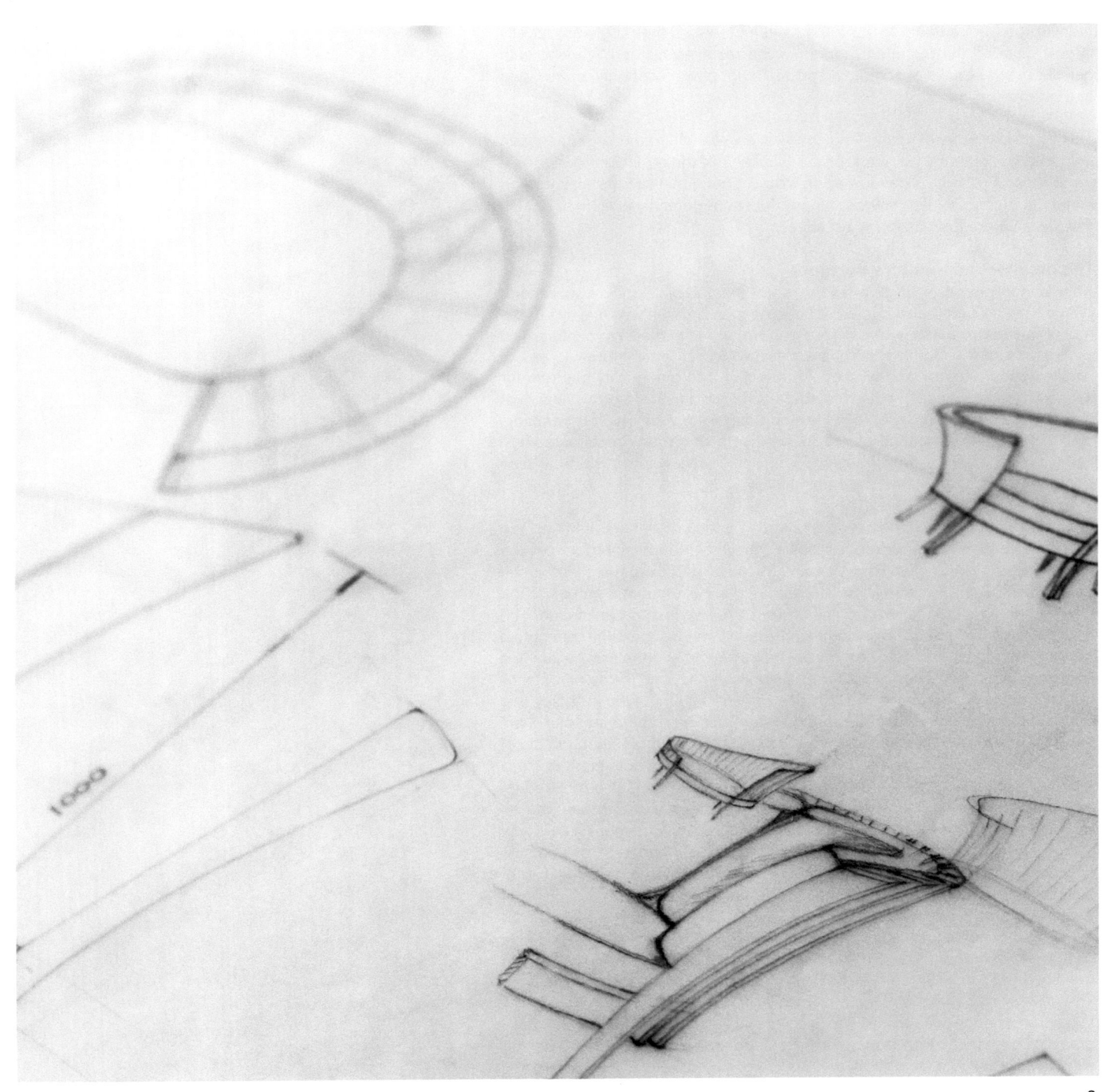

themselves were subject to the trends and methods of their day while royalty largely dictated the terms and therefore the resulting history. Working with oak today still speaks of something strong if not plain, functional, dominating and often anonymous.

This is but one story of many. To gain the overview, where the larger narrative helps us understand the work of Ed Cruikshank today, including his own personalised use of oak, we need to take a brief survey of the makers and materials during the last few centuries - focusing primarily on Great Britain, the place where Ed was born and raised.

The architect as furniture designer
After a long period of English history when memorable furniture was made primarily by a kind of royal decree (where the craftsperson was mainly but the tool of their patron) a new kind of designer appeared in the 17th century. The emergence of the Brithish merchant class added an entirely new group of wealthy people to the land who could now afford to buy quality furniture for their own little castles. As equal members of this new money, the architects of the day had a much broader, even level playing field, with which to practice. Not needing the patronage of a duke here or a king there, architects were being called on by a growing group of people who wanted the best they could buy, designed by the stars of their day.

In this way though, both the new patronage and their designers didn't fall too far from the blue blooded tree. As design movements transitioned from the ruling class driven English Renaissance, Palladian and Baroque styles to the upper class Georgian and Victorian, the inherent pretentious nature of the emerging architectural class continued to decree style and application. The architects of this period even templated their furniture ideas in catalogues which defined the must have's of their day. Nevertheless, a unified approach between the architecture of these homes and the furniture they contained began to appear. Builders like Sir William Chambers not only had the skills to construct the overall grandeur of estates such as Somerset House, he drew on various Asian influences in his attention to the minute details of latticed chair backs or ornate mirrors (following improvements in plate glass manufacturing). Another architect of the day, Robert Adam, also focused on home furnishings by drawing on his travels to France and Italy instilling an ornamental application to woodwork in furniture which was completely new to England at the time. These architects had an overall vision of both the structure of the home and it's furnishings which often co-opted the style of their travels. In this way, not only were the chairs, sideboards and beds of the period cleverly derivative, they were presented to the home owner as en vogue - no questions asked. Nowhere in this conversation was there a sense of true collaboration. The players had changed but the rules of the game remained the same.

What did change was access to a kind of bespoke furniture for a larger group of people. Not en masse, but a broadening of the market in keeping with the times. The emphasis of design remained within the imagination of the architect and not a collaboration necessarily with the purchaser. Nevertheless, movement was afoot.

The merchant craftsman as furniture designer

As the architects of the 17th and 18th centuries grew in popularity, they required equally skilled joiners and carpenters to produce the many pieces installed in the stately manors and homes they were building. As part of the era's ever growing merchant class, furniture makers like Robert Gillow (Gillow & Co.) were importing new materials like Satinwood and Mahogany from the Americas and West Indies which would compliment the style of the day while adding new possibilities for decoration. New techniques and skills for the creation of inlay and veneers not only gave voice to the architects overall vision, they became a springboard for the furniture manufacturers themselves to stand on the same pedestal. Gillow & Co started exporting their own designs back to the Americas and West Indies, ironically, and grew in the public eye as worthy trendsetters in their own right, able to supply stylish furniture sans the architect.

Part of this design transition was born of frustration, as was the case with the memorable Josiah Wedgwood, who despite the lack of appreciation from the architects of his day, would press on to make stunning jasperware friezes applied onto their chimney pieces nonetheless. Most of this transition from architect to craftsman (joiners, upholsters, carpenters) however, came from the combination of the continued growth of the middle and upper classes of England and the outstanding skills (finally being recognised as cohorts in design) of the 'new' furniture designers. These talented entrepreneurs not only brought foreign design ideas into the English home, they wrote their own books on design, sourced exotic materials and either kept up with or created entirely new technologies with which to complete furniture visions of their own.

For ages, carpenters and joiners were well versed in the idea of enduring quality. Getting their commissions from royalty or their suppliers raised the bar on design and build quality such that the norm for a chair or table would be that it remained beautiful and would last for generations. Interestingly, even as designers such as Thomas Chippendale began to template his creations in carpentry books and journals, they were still built in such a way that each structural piece, the materials used and joining technologies employed would outlive the man and his customer many times over. As the 18th and 19th centuries progressed, furniture designers also got closer and closer to the ones being designed for. Perhaps it was the social proximity of the carpenter to his customers (doctors, professors, bankers etc.) or their less pretentious nature - bred of being told what to make all the time - that lessened the gap. While there was still some crossover from the previous era of design control, carpenters and upholsterers started defining the style of the day while also being willing to customise and improve on their work through collaboration. In his seminal book - The Gentleman's and Cabinate Makers Director (note the word 'Director' - old habits…), Chippendale wrote "… I am confident I can convince all Noblemen, Gentlemen, or others who will honour me with their Commands, that every design in the book can be improved, both as to Beauty and Enrichment, in the execution of it, by Their most obedient servant,".

Of course, designers such as Chippendale, Robert Manwaring (who also published his own book), J. Mayhew and George Hepplewhite still defined most of the terms of the collaboration - as Hepplewhite pronounces in his book of over 300 designs "of every article of household furniture in the newest and most approved taste" - they nevertheless moved the connection between the chair and those who sat on it just a tad closer. Overall, who could complain? The outstanding level of construction, carving and build quality from these master craftsman continues to bring deep appreciation and unprecedented prices at auction to this day, some 250 years on. It may be said that the greater the craft, the greater the art and therefore collaboration is actually unnecessary. But as the power of the buyer increased and their connection to a larger pool of makers expanded, something had to give.

The inventor / cultural commentator as furniture designer
As the British Empire's influence on the world went into decline, the rest of the worlds influence on design became more apparent, even within English speaking culture. Of course, influences from China, Japan, Italy, Greece, Egypt and most importantly France had always impacted the design of furniture in Great Britain. However, the self proclaimed makers of fashion were still largely within 'the Empire', at least to the English way of thinking. This isn't to say that furniture designers, architects or even the royalty of the 17th through 19th centuries did not appreciate the amazing skills of foreign artists, but that the co-opting of their skill and style became so embedded within English design history, that naturally, as the Empire's influence waned the true influence of the larger world came into focus. Looking at the 20th century then, the design movement that stands out the most comes from the Continent and surprisingly perhaps, from Germany.

In the Bauhaus of the early 1920's, Walter Gropius - an architect himself - began to challenge the separation of architecture and furniture design by gathering students from an array of creative disciplines. Gropius started a movement in this way that by evoking the persona of his school, Bauhaus created furniture which was both industrial and playful at the same time. The interaction of faculty and student designers, new materials and emerging technologies, created a facsimile of collaboration with the end user in mind, but only within the microcosm of the outlandishly effective studio. The Bauhaus idea was not to create a particularly modern style of the times, but a way of living that stripped back the frills of the preceding Art Nouveau period so that the highest value could be placed in making functional objects for the largest number of people. The resulting genius of Bauhaus designers such as Marcel Breuer and his Model B3 Chair (also known as the Wassily Chair) shows a clear connection between a modernists industrial sense of infrastructure and the desired citizen of the new age.

Paradigm shifts in furniture design started to pick up pace here. Technological developments accelerated allowing an even broader range of techniques, made accessible to a broadening group of designers and therefore their customers. The wars of this century propelled national design movements forward in the same way that the royalty of previous centuries pushed the design envelope, albeit at a snails pace. A democratisation of both design manufacturing and the resulting product ethos moved design of the 20th century from ego driven mandates to a philosophical platform, especially seen through steel or plastic creations. Not that ego took a back seat, but for the furniture designer of this era, materials, technologies, philosophies and customers all expanded at breakneck speed blurring the notion that anyone was actually in control.

Still, without the networks and value chains of the 21st century, designers were still focusing, as they had for centuries, on what they could produce in-house, then pitching their wares to the impressionable customer. While studios in Germany, Sweden and the U.S. got more intwined within their playful, creative inner worlds, their connection with the customer become more and more an issue of marketing rather than conversation.

The artist as furniture designer
As it was likely to do, the industrial modernist view of life was bound to give way to a more humane, even organic approach to design. As industry got uglier, designers became more committed to the art of their craft while maintaining a connection to technology in order to fulfil their dreams. One such dream was the moulding of plywood to comply with the human form, the way leather would, say, on a saddle. Charles Eames had this bright idea while at school in the late 1930's and spent decades perfecting it. As an architect, industrial designer and definitely as an artist, Charles - and later with Ray Eames - created a wide array of pieces from household furniture to Worlds Fair installations which displayed their artistic / humane approach to design. This approach resonated deeply within an international psyche in need of both connection and conversation.

Collaboration within the Eames' studio was at the same time both inclusive and singular. Like the Bauhaus, the Eames' labs would collect people from various disciplines to create their pieces, but largely under the control of Charles. This artistic approach hints at a kind of connection with the potential customer, but is mostly held back by Ruskin's precept where "The first condition of a work of art is that it should be conceived and carried out by one person". The gorgeous and highly functional 'mid century' furniture that came from the world of Eames, and that of similar designers including Arne Jacobsen, continued to add a humane element to the modern world while very much keeping to their own visions of that world. Taking the artistic stance in furniture design even further, Verner Panton bridged technology and art in the creation of his signature chair, moulded entirely from a single piece of plastic, appropriately named - The S Chair.

The furniture designer as artists definitely pushed the field forward but not necessarily towards the end user. Style and ego continued to interact with materials and technologies but the concept of bespoke remained within the narrow space between the artist and the gallery. What grew however was a growing sense of possibility for the designer, who with an ever expanding palate of ideas and methods with which to create, could move beyond the constraints of centuries of design while benefitting from all that went before them, if they cared to.

21st century furniture design
With unprecedented access to the details of history, the furniture designer of this century has the ability to both pay attention to these stories while developing their own sense of style and purpose. The challenge they face, as did their predecessors, is whether they will pay attention to their customers. The design dilemma of the ages seems to be whether to create from a very internal, even narrow space (either through commissions or self-made projects), or to collaborate and bridge the gap between design and use - between an object and the very people who will extend it's story as owners.

We've seen from Sir William Chambers that furniture can be connected - if not constrained - by a larger architectural vision which seems to create a legacy, but more in terms of historical posterity rather than a family space enjoyed for centuries. We've seen from Chippendale that pure craft can create highly valuable, long lasting, beautiful chairs that God forbid, anyone should actually sit on. Of course, in his day, people did, but there is a sense that the more 'elegant' a piece of furniture is, the less one should actually interact with it. We've seen from Breuer and Eames that technology and beauty can come together in a very functional, even comfortable way which you and two million other people can all enjoy at the same time thanks to the manufacturing skills of companies such as Herman Miller. What does not seem obvious throughout the last few centuries is an intentional conversation between highly skilled and sought after furniture designers and the ones being designed for. There are of course some stories of this kind, but they are so few are far between that modern design movements, school curricula and apprenticeships today make little mention of them.

This is where Cruikshank enters the narrative and pushes the story forward, if just a bit, in his own way. The quality of his work is not of singular genius, but the ability to know, adopt from and personalise these larger stories into a particular narrative that both speaks to and suits the furniture's owner. The three owners if you will. For Ed, who owns the skill and results of his work, his story is an evolving connection with his education, craft and a bond with his customers, most of whom become friends. For the buyer, who owns the collaboration process and the resulting piece of furniture, their story becomes a kind of time piece, where the furniture both reflects those historical tells while slowly ticking away towards a future marked by the lovely patina of use. For the piece itself, which embeds this collection of histories and will likely outlive both Cruikshank and customer, it's story is briefly catalogued in this book. A simple visual clue, each piece allowing the reader the opportunity to travel through time, past and present, considering their own legacy via connections to these beautiful objects of furniture.

Ed Cruikshank lives and designs in the Queenstown Lakes region of New Zealand's South Island. An environment rich in colour, texture and inspiration. The designs before you are as connected to the land Ed dwells in as they are to the people he designs for.

27

HERBRITTS

RUSCHA EDITIONS 1959-1999

CATALOGUE RAISONNÉ

TING S
ME ON
8-1970

40

BORDEAU

88

89

102

119

120

As Cruikshank is fond of thinking hundreds of years ahead, to explore his interest in coded language we need to look more than 200 years back, to a time when blindness and battle were more common than they are today. In modern times, where our computer screens glow with blue light in the darkness and any manner of device can read us the written word, we forget how challenging life could have been if one hoped to communicate silently in the dark, or worse, if one lived in perpetual darkness.

At the outset of the 19th century, a French Artillery officer named Charles Barbier invented a raised dot system of phonetic communication for soldiers who needed to pass messages to each other in the dark. Complex, using configurations of 12 raised dots for the letters, it proved useful but difficult. A few years later, a 15 year old student at the Paris School for the Blind, modified Barbier's system to configurations of 6 raised dots. The young student's name would become synonymous with the coded language he created, and for nearly 200 years Louis Braille's system of embossed dots that could be read by fingertips has become the predominant written language for the blind. Other coded and raised letters had been

developed in the 19th century too, each with its own specialty. Moon type, for instance, was larger curved, and was easily mastered by those who had once been sighted, but very difficult to reproduce in books. Boston Line Type was the favorite of the Perkins School for the Blink in Boston and was used by Helen Keller, but it required expensive tools to duplicate or for people to engage in writing with it. Only Braille proved universal, affordable, and practical.

It is also, to the untrained hand and eye, mysterious and almost mathematical. Like Morse Code, which would come later with the invention of the telegraph, these systems of dots and dashes were a way of communicating differently. Oddly enough, the people who first put their hands on the walls of El Castillo may have been far more comfortable with a system of raised dots than we are, as many of the caves in Europe have panels created of circular thumb and finger dots which likely were forms of communication and speak to something we cannot understand. Like Braille, when we see it, but cannot decipher it, the mystery tugs at us and asks us to look more intimately and to go deeper.

Not all of Cruikshank's works contain intimacies, but many do. His foray into Braille began with an invitation in 2010 from art collector, patron and friend David Teplitzky, who asked Cruikshank to participate in an art exhibition called Roundabout held initially at the Wellington City Gallery and later in Tel Aviv where it drew record crowds. In response to the theme of the exhibition, he designed his 1821 table with 108 pieces to correspond with the 108 artists who came together to share their work. Each choice in the piece, from the walnut wood and the gun blue metal, the same metal and wood used in guns, amplified and emphasized the theme that he encoded in the center of the table. Using an inverted braille where neither blind nor sighted would be advantaged in interpreting it, he encoded Martin Luther King's immortal words, "I have decided to stick with love, hate is too great a burden to bear." By using materials usually associated with the manufacture of firearms as parts of an object that unifies, literally bringing people around the same table, Cruikshank hoped to instill a message of peace, tolerance and communication.

This initial foray into a deep intentionality in his work in terms of materials and communication has led Cruikshank on a journey of form and function where he has designed tables that are held together with bolts that spell Love in Braille, and the creation of tables whose legs have the names of each member of the family encoded within them so that the table is symbolically held up by the members of the family who sit around it. To the outside, the random patterns of holes are unique design. To the insider, the legs of the table hold deep and intimate symbolism. To future generations, it is not only a table, but an incarnation of the family tree.

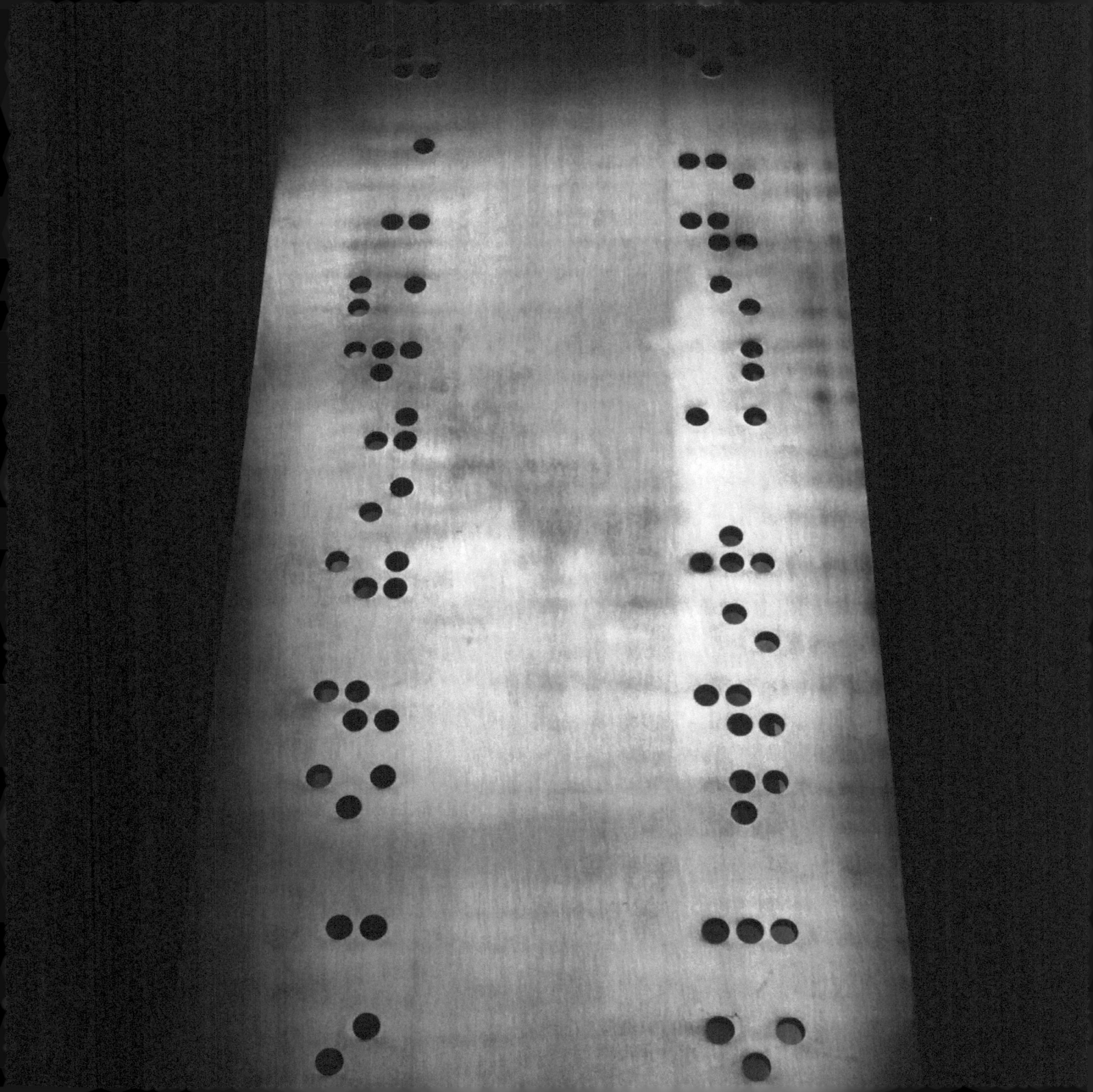

137

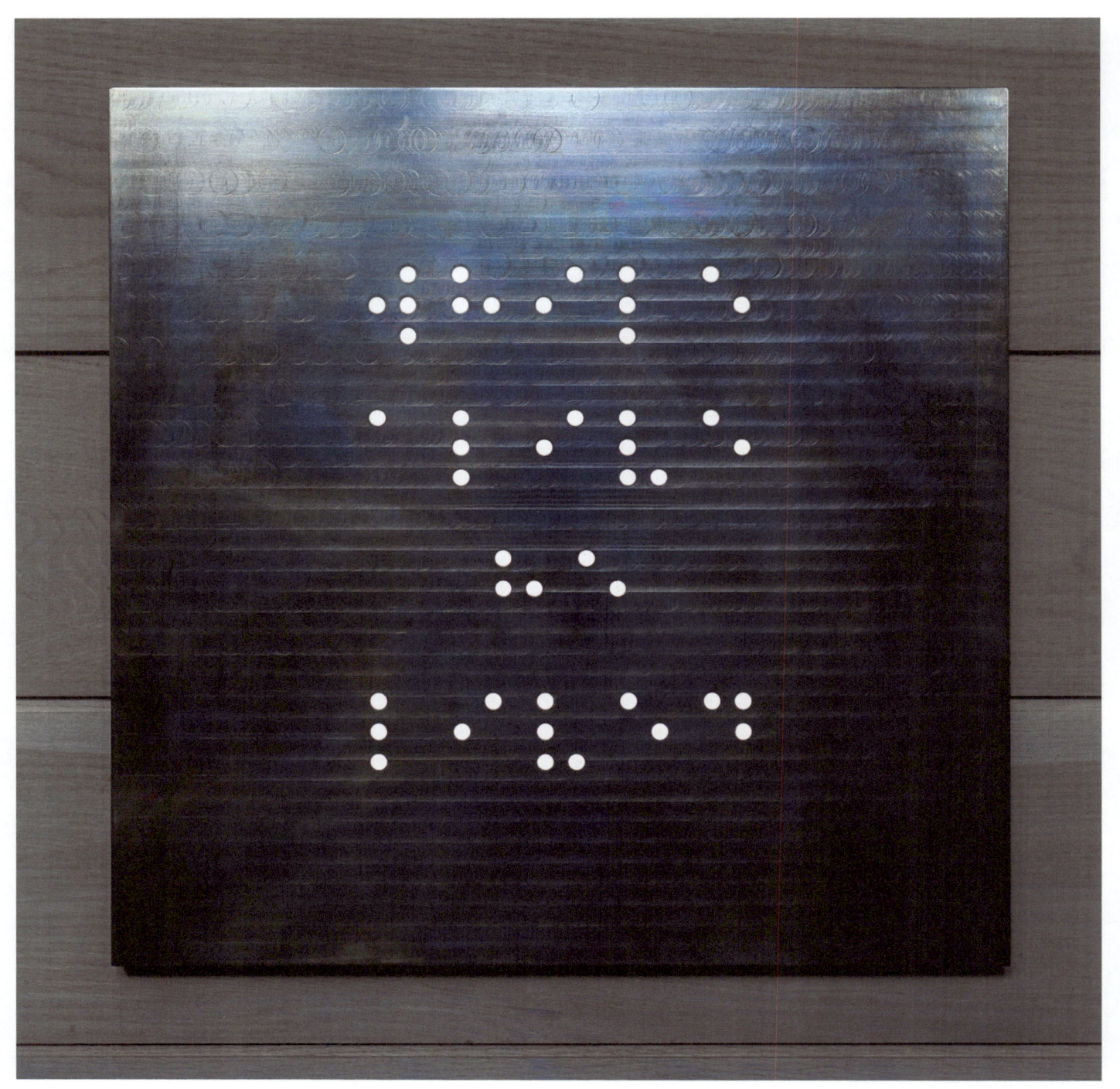

138

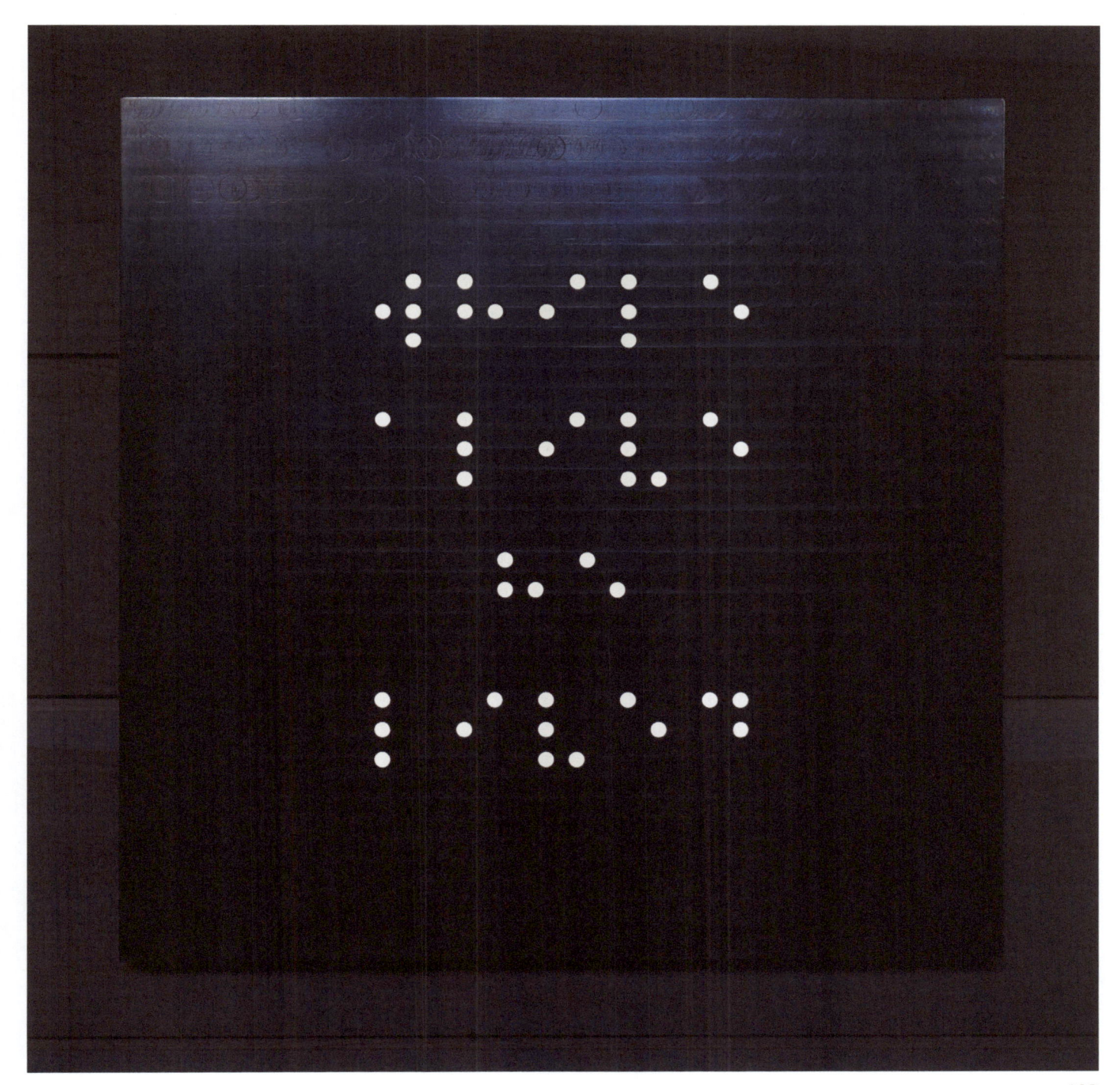

Simplicity from Ed's perspective

I like simplicity.

It can be described in many ways; elegance, perfection, clarity, integrity, purity, naturalness, openness, ease.

Like a silky-smooth pebble formed over millions of years, simplicity takes time to come into being. Gradual shaping, slow change, simplicity waits with infinite patience to slowly reveal itself.

Simplicity is in fact infinite complexity, distilled by the passage of time.

In simplicity beauty cannot help but exist too. Both are everywhere around us. Humankind continues to strive to understand their underlying nature, the mathematical and physical laws that govern everything in our universe - the movement of the planets, the tides, the aerodynamic lift of a birds wing, the form of a breaking wave or the gentle flow of a stream.

As a designer I am constantly aware of the relationship between complexity, simplicity and beauty. I strive to create objects that express some of these elusive qualities.

When I feel I am on the right path I am always struck not by a feeling of my own skill, but of a sense of tapping into a universal energy and intelligence. I liken it to allowing myself to float down a river, noticing details of the banks, the river bed and the sky as I pass, glimpsing them and attempting to record them in the stroke of a pencil or the line and balance of the design.

We often describe the best man-made things as timeless. We see it in architecture, art, music, furniture, sculpture, literature, food, wine and also stories.

When we detect timelessness I believe we are aware of, and are connecting with this universal matrix. Call it God or Spirit or Nature or Truth we sense a fleeting connection with something eternal, beyond description or possession.

Generally I think we regard man-made timelessness as something we can see, but in fact we access it equally through all of our senses. You only have to close your eyes listening to a beautiful piece of music or to know this.

For me, the tactility, smell, sound and weight of an object are equally important as the way it looks. The feeling of permanence created by weight, the reassurance of the crisp 'click' of a well-made latch, the physical satisfaction of sliding a drawer effortlessly to defined stop, the warm childhood memories and sense of history created by the scent of an old leather armchair. By closing our eyes we become aware of so much more.

The most wonderful sensual reaction to my furniture I ever experienced was the shriek of surprise and joy of a blind friend sitting in my Koru chair for the first time. For him the way the sound was absorbed, as if by new snow, and the sense and feeling of being enveloped and safe created a powerful emotional response.

It is challenging to try to describe the essence of ones work as it is always changing and evolving. As we gather knowledge, learn new skills, make mistakes, practice and hone our craft, we gradually build a unique creative vocabulary and landscape that manifests in the work itself.

I am keenly aware as I see and experience more that I am only just beginning to understand what it takes to be a good designer and that it will take the rest of my life to learn just a fraction more of what there is to be learned.

I am sure of one thing - that the intention behind my work is equal to and as worthy as any other designer's who came before or will follow me.

I know this because at the heart of my practice is a sincere intension of kindness. My greatest hope is that my furniture will simply give pleasure and comfort to the people who come into contact with it.

They say that old musical instruments subtly change as they are imbued with the memories of the music and the musicians they encounter.

I like to think that echoes of the lives and stories of all the people who use and enjoy my furniture are captured and stored within it and that their energy, love and kindness becomes part of the furniture itself, resonating in the present moment while simultaneously connecting with past and future generations.

This is why I put so much effort into the quality and longevity of what I produce. I believe it is also why an increasing number of my customers are attracted to the idea of embedding special personal meaning into the pieces.

143

144

My dad's clock

As a boy I was sometimes embarrassed by my father's often brusk manner. He didn't suffer fools and was always prepared to challenge unfairness and incompetence. At the same time he could be remarkably kind and generous. I realise now that he had a very strong sense of self.

Dad was a genius with his hands, an inventor and fixer of the unfixable. After retiring he threw himself into the world of clocks and watches, quickly becoming a Master of Horology and lecturing the students that he studied with the previous year.

He died just before Christmas 2014 after a long battle with Cancer. A year earlier, when the dreadful shadow returned following a period of remission, I decided that I wanted to make something with him, while we still had time.

I designed a clock using the same Walnut and gun-blued steel with indented Braille from my recent art pieces. Dad supplied the appropriate traditional movement to fit the case. We had both come a long way since our first joint effort - a birdhouse we made together when I was a little boy.

I still get a knot in my throat when I translate the Braille into words when people ask its meaning, but the tears that still well up are always accompanied by a smile and a feeling of gratitude for the time we spent and that we made it together.

Creating anything that connects us with other people is incredibly satisfying. It is what I love most about my job. I get to work closely with people and gain insight into their worlds and the things they care about most.

Home and family and are always at the top of the list and I am increasingly asked to embed or inscribe meaningful messages or texts into custom pieces. Encoded in Braille or Morse Code they predominantly relate to family, friends and loved ones, present, past and yet to be born.

152

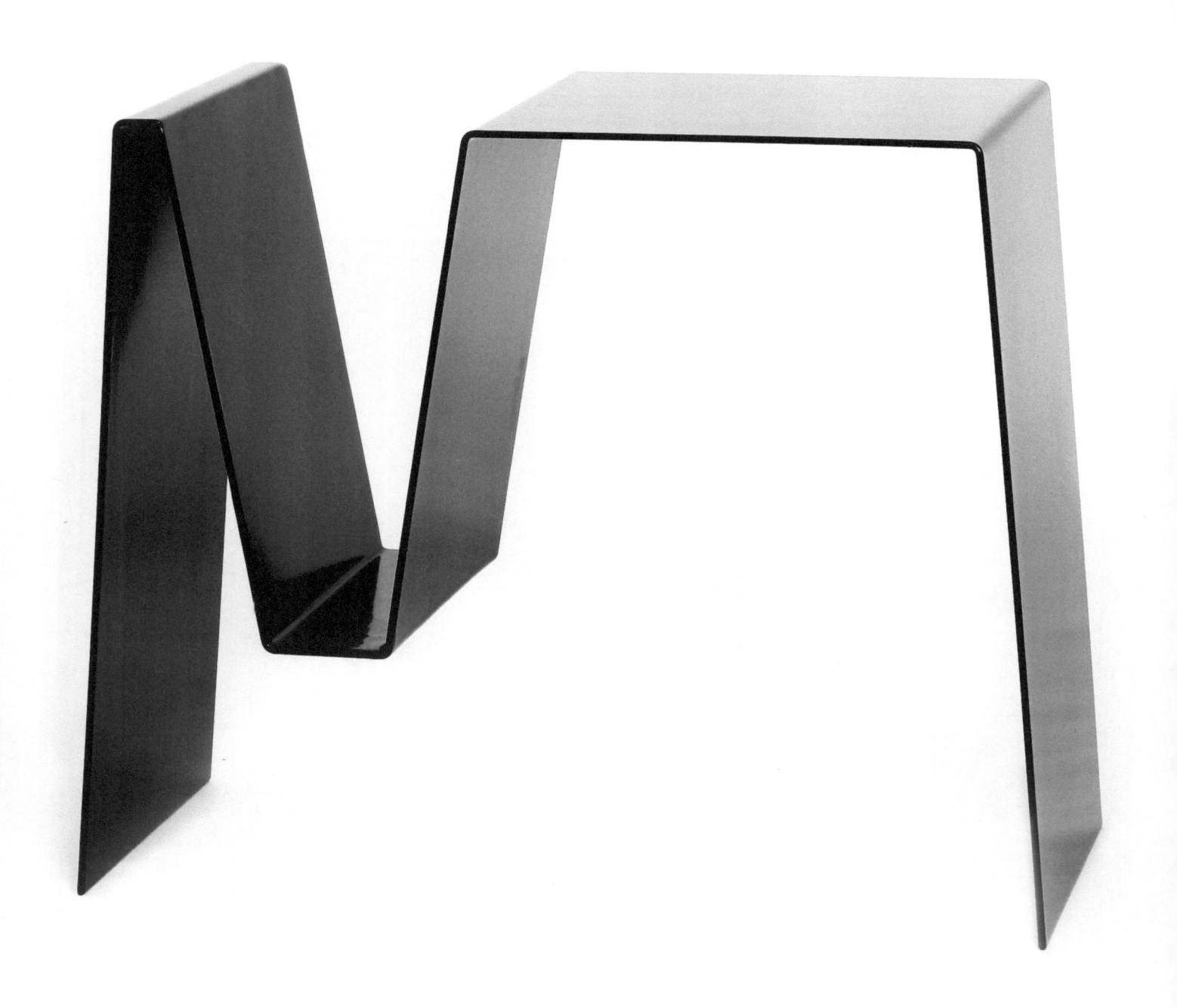

Craftsmenship

I don't believe we are born with an innate sense of craftsmanship or quality. Like everything else in life they are things we learn, a sensory language we develop as we explore our environment and discover the materials and techniques that combine to create them.

As a child I was surrounded by exquisitely-engineered objects that my father had either made or collected. Beautiful miniature steam engines, perfectly-made components and the intricate tools and precise machines that formed them.

My next memory of craftsmanship was through technical drafting at school. I was intrigued by geometry and the constructional techniques used to define three dimentional objects in two dimensions but most of all I loved the craft of the drawing itself, the care and precision needed to produce a clean, accurate and elegant result.

At cabinet-making school I came to understand what it is to make something extremely well. The pleasure of using a perfectly-sharpened chisel or plane, the thrill and satisfaction of cutting a faultless dove-tail joint. Whole days would flash by as I immersed myself the world of craftsmanship.

Learning the foundations of a craft and practicing the techniques creates accuracy and an understanding of the material. Applying the same care and attention to each detail, the whole piece of furniture gradually emerges. The sum of these perfect parts will enable it to remain intact and function properly for many years - even generations.

Design came to the fore in the next phase of my life while studying industrial design.
I learned that good design requires creativity and imagination and, in common with craftsmanship, it must be tempered with rigour and discipline. Clever, intelligently designed things can have a powerful influence on the way we live and how we interact with our environment but if they are not well crafted they will not stand the tests of time and the ingenuity, beauty and meaning of the design will be lost.

During my time in London working with David Linley, I studied and was surrounded by, wonderful classical and contemporary works of art, design and architecture. I was constantly amazed by their quality, endurance and ingenuity.

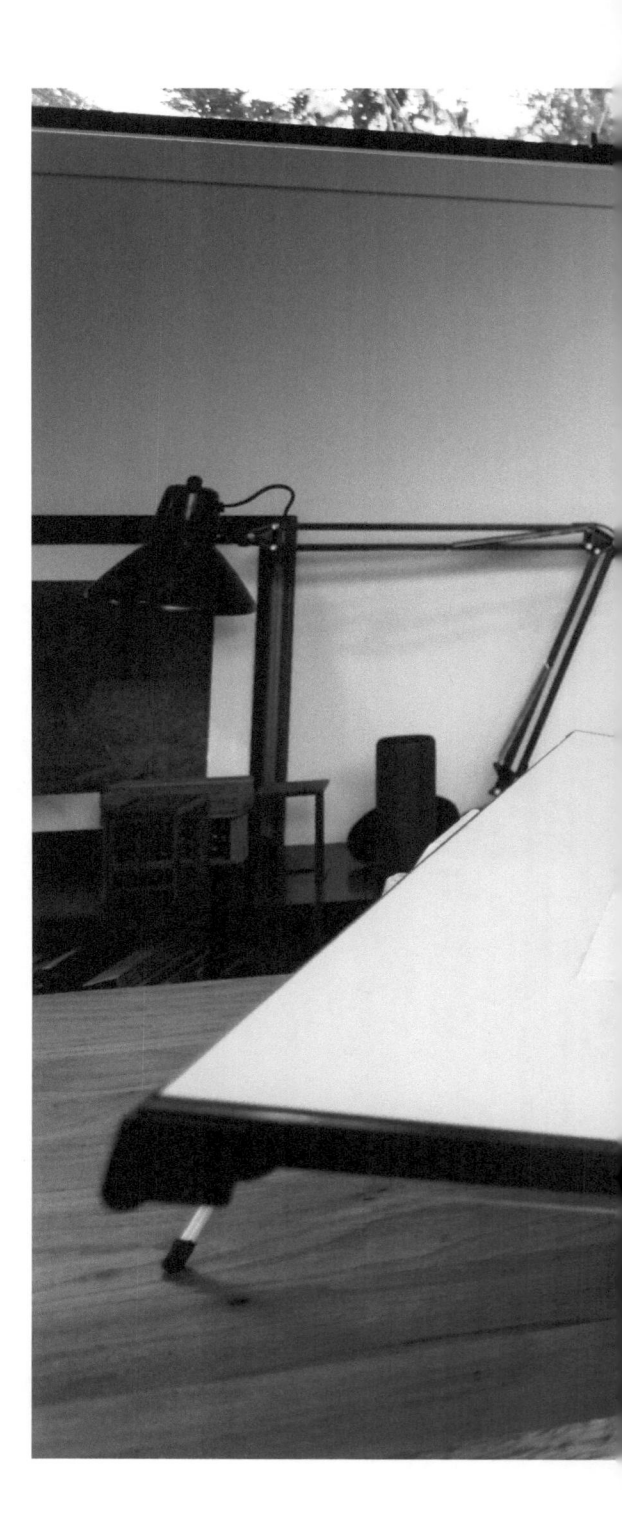

I would regularly reach a frustrating impass while working on a complicated or challenging detail for a new design and would take a break from the drawing board to wander along Pimlico Road, calling in for a cups of tea with the various antique shop owners to see if they could help. They would usually show me a wonderfully elegant and simple version of the detail I was struggling with, already several hundred years old and still working perfectly. I was fortunate to work with some of the world's most talented craftspeople who built the custom pieces we were designing. They were experts in their field and I spent many fascinating days visiting them at their workshops in lovely parts of England and elsewhere in Europe to discuss the best way to make the piece. Many of the companies had been in business for several generations and are still building Linley pieces today

A passion for building things properly - so that they will last - is always at the core of these businesses and is the reason they thrive and endure. Through great craftsmanship even the simplest object becomes more than the sum of the parts. The care and energy imparted by the craftspeople lifts the object to another level where even the simplest items become works of art in their own right.

My own designs are usually simple. I use high quality materials, clean lines and clearly-expressed structure. Junctions and connections are key feautures and the eye is drawn to and scrutinises these details, so the execution and craftsmanship is vital to the success of the piece.

There are also many great craftsmen here in New Zealand. The ones I work with have been in business for several generations. We understand each other and I continue to enjoy working with them fifteen years after making our first pieces.
In the same way I enjoy welcoming back customers from those early years who return again and again to experience and often extend our levels of craftsmanship and design.

I hope that the pieces I create, influenced by all of my own experiences and crafted using the skills and knowledge of previous generations will endure to bring pleasure and enjoyment for many years to come.

182

184

My story

I was born in the North West of England in 1965. I grew up in a small village surrounded by farmland and woods where I spent a very free and simple childhood with seemingly endless days playing with friends in the fields, climbing ridiculously tall trees and biking the quiet lanes. It was a happy time.

My father was a skilled electrical engineer with IBM at a time when computers were still machines with moving parts. He worked long hours, dedicated to fixing the things his colleagues had given up on. My mother did the incredible job of keeping our big Victorian home and raising four boisterous children – probably the harder of the two jobs.

I always remember Dad's story of a visiting big-wig from America telling him and several hundred of his wide-eyed colleagues, "That one day a computer will exist with over one Gigabyte of memory (gasp) and gentlemen, it will fit in a space no bigger than this very conference room".
How times change!

Dad's passion for machines would have spilled out from his garden workshop into every corner of our home had mum not banned his oily contraptions from the house.

My older sister and brother followed dad's scientific lead, becoming doctors and mechanical engineers as did my younger brother later on.
Somehow I navigated my way through the UK 's 'O' and 'A' level school curricula, generally exercising my social rather than academic skills. The subjects that I seemed to do best in – possibly to the dismay of my parents - were technical drawing and art.

I managed to scrape through with passes in the sciences and a couple of A's in the more artistic subjects and departed Appleton Hall County Grammar School non-the-wiser about my next move. I decided to knuckle down and went skiing for a season in the French Alps.

After returning strong-legged and sun-burnt several seasons later, I started to think about applying myself to something constructive, when out of the blue, an opportunity for a place at a cabinet making course presented itself. I went for an interview armed with my school folio of technical drawings and sketches. Before I knew it I was at Rycotewood College in Thame near Oxfordshire - a heaven of craftsmanship and country pubs.

I loved making things and I realised that I always had, but had never considered it as a potential career – a way to literally make a living. But it was design that really hooked me.

After finishing the cabinet-making course I continued on my creative path and

186

took the train to London for an interview at the superb art and design college Ravensbourne, loaded up with various crafted objects and a thicker portfolio of drawings and designs.

Three years later, just before attaining an honours degree in industrial furniture design, I was snapped up by the rather exciting if slightly scary-sounding Viscount Linley to work as a link between his Kings Road design studio and West Country workshops. A perfect position to make the most of my five years of training.

So this small town boy suddenly found himself at the sharp end of global high society working for and with some of big names in the design, showbiz and pretty much every other world you could thing of.

To be honest it was terrifying at first. Even the lovely company secretary was scary, in a very beautiful, posh way. There were regular parties where my colleagues and I were tasked with schmoosing the great and the good guests who were always in attendance. Famous actors, rock stars, heads of state, royalty, sporting legends - it was mind-blowing.

I will never forget one hot summer evening slipping out from one of these gatherings to get some fresh air and realising I had just brushed past Princess Diana and Margaret Thatcher.

Standing in the cool side street, out of sight of the resident Papparazzi, I was suddenly cornered by a Bond-like royal security guard who had appeared out of thin air.
"Evening Sir, do you mind me asking what you are doing here?"
Before answering I clearly remember thinking that it was a very good question.

A year or so later, at a similar event, I had a revelation that changed me for good.
I had been chatting and drinking a little too much with an extremely suave Italian and his hilarious, slightly disheveled aristocratic friend when David Linley tapped me on the shoulder and said 'Cruiky...leave these two alone and do some mingling'.
I said goodbye to my new friends and rejoined the throng.

I was soon approached by a couple of sharp-suited bankers who had brushed me off earlier in the evening when they had realised I was from north of Sloane Square.
'Do you think you could introduce us to your friends?'.
'Who?' I asked.
'X and Lord X of course'.
I smiled and asked if they had ever been to Manchester.

It was at that moment that it became crystal clear to me that no matter what situation and what company you find yourself, being yourself and speaking honestly and openly opens up a world of infinite possibility and sets you on a level playing field with every other human being, regardless of their position or background.

Five or so years later, still loving my job in London, I came to New Zealand for the first time whilst designing the interior of a beautiful sloop being built in Auckland for a Linley customer. I loved the landscape and beauty of New Zealand but what impressed me most was the attitude and character of the Kiwis. I knew I had found a special place.

Each time I flew down during the course of the project I would add a week to my trip to see more of the country. During my last visit, after the launch of the yacht, I came to Queenstown for the first time.

Sitting drinking a coffee on the wharf I had a powerful sense that the town would somehow play a significant part in my future.

Two years later and back in my London life, I reconnected with an old friend from my alpine days. We had taught skiing in Switzerland during our college time and had both been in London for about ten years since. That Christmas we were both in France on separate ski trips and caught up by coincidence. We had a great day skiing and chatting away on the chair lift. She said she was off to Sydney for a break from a stressful Accident and Emergency post at St Thomas's Hospital and some time away from the hectic London lifestyle.

Several months later I was reading a lovely book by the extraordinary Irish poet and philosopher John O'Donohue. It had a profound effect on me at a time when I was feeling unsettled and in need of a new perspective.

Remembering a conversation we had in France, I dropped my friend a line in Sydney to say hello and, having just finished reading it, I enclosed the book hoping she would find it interesting too. A few weeks later an email arrived saying how much she had enjoyed it and a conversation that would entwine us and take us on an incredible adventure and a life on the opposite side of the world began.

With some sadness but also great excitement, I resigned from my position with Linley. I had many good friends there and leaving was a big step. Lots of people told me I was crazy to leave one of the best furniture design jobs in London. But I had made up my mind. I felt slightly better when David gave me a boomerang as a parting gift though.

Tonya and I spent a year or so in Australia, just north of Sydney on the beautiful Central Coast and had many adventures around the country. We had always planned to return to England, Tonya would continue her medical training and I would perhaps return to Linley but we wanted to see New Zealand and do some skiing first so we did some research and Tonya found a seasonal job, working as a ski field doctor in a little place called Queenstown.

The plan was to stay for three months. There was unlikely to be any work for me in such an out of the way place so I decided to improve my skiing and train to be an instructor.

After two months or so I started to get itchy fingers and went looking for cabinet-makers to see if they had any casual work. I was offered some part time work and, as we were both enjoying Queenstown so much we decided to extend our stay.

I soon realised there was far more to Queenstown than I had thought. Interesting people were commissioning great architects to build beautiful homes and they were looking for custom furniture.

I decided to investigate. I bought a drawing board and the other tools I needed to start designing again. The first job led to another then another and before long I had my own business.

I set up in Arrowtown a few years later where I had a great little shop and design studio. In 2015 I decided to change tack to focus purely on the custom projects that I love. I built a small private studio at our home with views of the magnificent mountains all around where I spend whole days designing, focused and undisturbed.

Here in this beautiful place that I call home, I sometimes recall being asked at cabinet-making school if I had a goal? I have never considered my self ambitious but I remember being struck at the time by an answer that popped into my head out of the blue – "To have a design studio in a ski resort".

To consciously put oneself in the flow of the long expanse of time is to risk anonymity for the possibility of endurance. We do not know the name of the people who first put their hands on the cave walls, and yet their image crosses time to inspire us today. We do not know the moment that the Kauri tree fell and how it came to rest beneath the waters for over thirty thousand years only to re-emerge in this century to tell its story again. Hundreds of years from now, will people still read Braille and know that Cruikshank's table has love as its center? Will the stories of the scratches in the leather of his chairs bear names or only be reminders that each life is filled with stories and that furniture captures and holds these intimacies, offering them again and again to each generation anew.

Cruikshank is at peace with the anonymity of time because he welcomes the evolving future and the story yet untold. To him, what matters most is the delight people have known in his pieces now and the knowledge that made from the materials of the earth, they will endure and grow softer, smoother, and more richly storied in the long expanse of time to come.

Lightning Source UK Ltd.
Milton Keynes UK
UKHW051135260820
368583UK00020B/14